The Ultimate MARKETING PLANNER for Children's Book Authors

Work One Week, Profit All Month

Created by Diana Aleksandrova

Paperback ISBN: 978-1-953118-41-7

Spiral Bound ISBN: 978-1-953118-42-4

For more additional resources and free downloadable templates, visit dedonibooks.com/resources

Published by Dedoni Books

Work One Week, Profit All Month

The Ultimate
MARKETING PLANNER
for Children's Book Authors

Work One Week, Profit All Month

This planner is designed to help you efficiently manage your marketing efforts with a streamlined approach to ongoing tasks and a structured plan for weekly activities.

It's ideal for authors who prefer to focus their marketing efforts in a concentrated, dedicated week each month. Dedicate one week a month to schedule everything from social media posts and email campaigns to essential tasks that keep your marketing consistent and engaging.

For the rest of the month, you can focus on writing, creating, and other priorities while your marketing operates smoothly in the background.
This planner provides a comprehensive approach to managing your marketing efforts.

How to Use This Planner:

One Week Per Month: Dedicate the first week of each month to complete the tasks for that month's focus area.

Automation: Where possible, automate tasks to ensure ongoing engagement without additional time investment.

Track Progress: Use the planner to track your progress on each task and reflect on what worked well.

Improve and Adjust: Regularly review your results, refine your approach, and make necessary changes.

Some tasks, like creating and scheduling social media posts, will remain the same each month. Others, like adjusting your blurbs and updating your email automation, will vary.

Things to do every month:
Replying to emails
Replying to messages or comments on social media posts
Engage with at least five other accounts by commenting on their posts or sharing their content
Adjusting Amazon Ads
Creating and scheduling social media posts
Email newsletter for the month

3-6 months tasks
Update Target personas
Improve Blurb
Update A-content if needed
Email automation adjustment
Running Free Promos
Updating Marketing Materials

Before you can develop and execute a successful marketing plan, you need to establish a solid foundation.

Begin by identifying your book's unique qualities—the elements that set it apart and are good selling points.

Next, identify and get to know your target audience (those buyers who are most likely to become your customers) by creating a detailed customer persona.

Then, create a marketing message that resonates with your target audience.

Set up your website, social media, and Email Service Provider.

Don't worry; you will be guided every step of the way.

If you have already completed a step (like having a website) and are happy with the result, move to the next task. You can always go back and improve.

Title of the book:

Genre and intended age group:

_____

What is your book about? What is the message?

_____
_____
_____
_____
_____
_____
_____

What do others say your book is about?

_____
_____
_____
_____
_____
_____
_____
_____
_____
_____
_____

What problems does your book solve? How does it help readers?

_____

_____

_____

_____

_____

Does your book fit in a niche?

_____

_____

Do your "survey." Study your book's reviews on Amazon and Goodreads. Write down the positive comments and phrases readers say about your book. That will help you craft and improve your blurb.

_____

_____

_____

_____

_____

_____

_____

_____

_____

_____

_____

_____

Find successful books similar to yours and read their reviews. This will help you understand what buyers are looking for.

Title:_____ by:_____
Title:_____ by:_____
Title:_____ by:_____
Title:_____ by:_____
Title:_____ by:_____
Title:_____ by:_____
Title:_____ by:_____
Title:_____ by:_____
Title:_____ by:_____
Title:_____ by:_____

Write down positive comments and phrases used in the reviews of those books that can be used in your blurb:

_____

_____

_____

_____

_____

_____

_____

_____

_____

_____

_____

_____

What categories does your book belong to? List all categories and select the most suitable one. Currently, Amazon allows only three categories for new books.

_____

_____

_____

_____

_____

_____

_____

_____

_____

_____

KDP Keywords:

_____

_____

_____

_____

_____

_____

_____

_____

_____

_____

_____

_____

Notes:

Customer Persona:

Define your target audience. Give your customer persona a name (parent, teacher, etc.) What is their relationship to the child?

Child's interests:

_____
_____
_____
_____

Child's struggles:

_____
_____
_____

Customer's challenges:

_____
_____
_____

Customer's goals:

_____
_____
_____

Where do they get their recommendations from?

_____

_____

_____

Where do they shop?

_____

_____

_____

Preferred book features:

_____

_____

_____

_____

Other important information about your customer:

_____

_____

_____

_____

_____

_____

_____

_____

Marketing message:

_____

_____

_____

_____

_____

_____

_____

_____

_____

_____

_____

_____

_____

_____

_____

_____

_____

_____

_____

_____

_____

_____

_____

_____

_____

_____

_____

_____

_____

Use this space to write down your most-used HASHTAGS.
You can easily refer to the list and add new ones over time.

_____

_____

_____

_____

_____

_____

_____

_____

_____

_____

_____

_____

_____

_____

_____

_____

_____

_____

_____

_____

_____

_____

_____

_____

_____

_____

_____

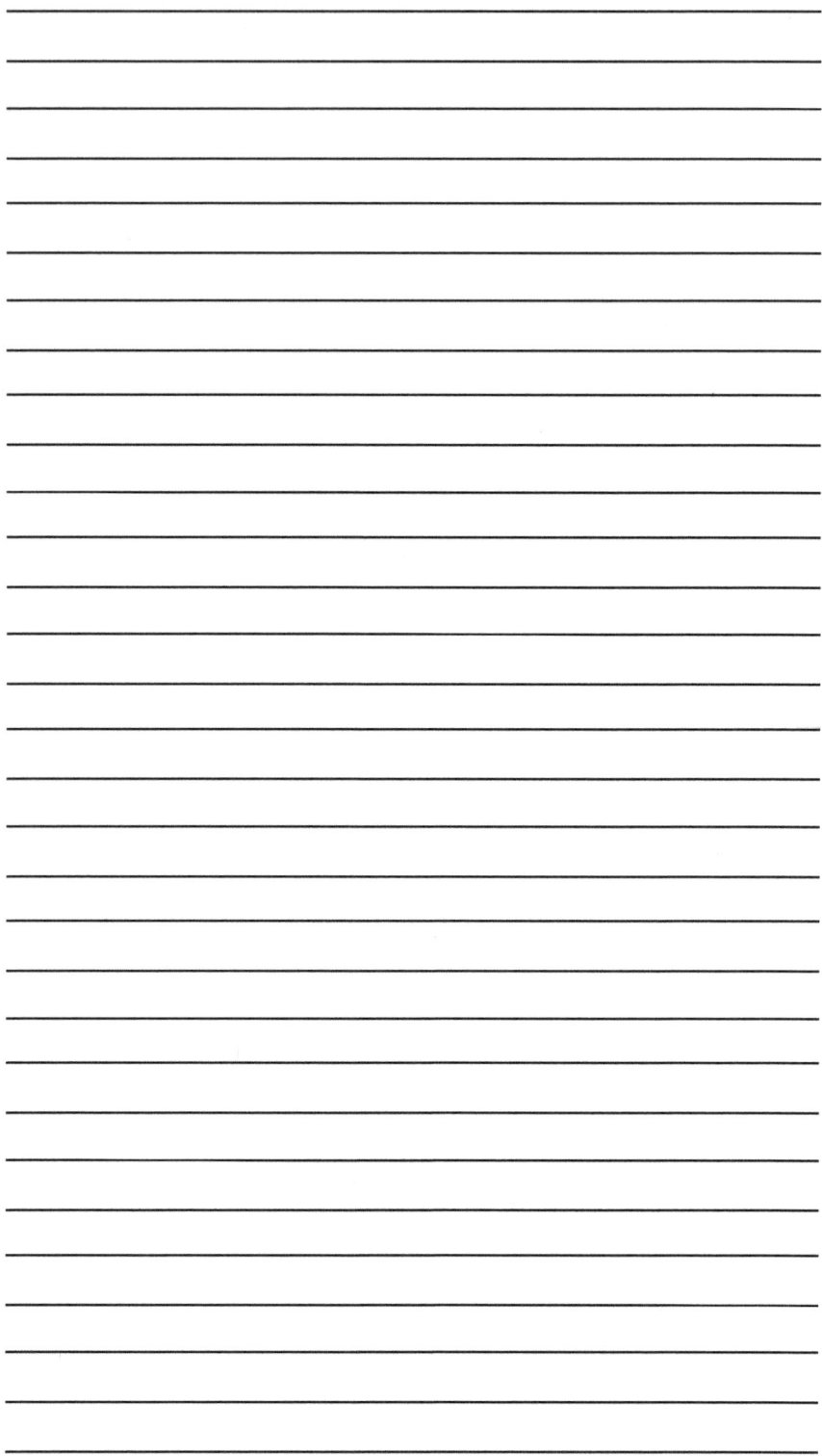

Make sure your website is user-friendly. Include titles and descriptions for all pages. Confirm you have all the essential elements:

About the Author

Books

Contact Information

Blog (if you are writing one)

Newsletter sign-up forms (pop-up and embedded forms)

Links to your social media.

Include a Press Kit: In addition to your media kit, develop a full press kit that includes a press release, author bio, high-resolution images, and a fact sheet about your book.

Create your Amazon Author Page. Claim your books. If you have one already, update your bio and recommendations.

Claim your books on Goodreads. If you already have an account, update your bio and recommendations. Then, link your blog to your Goodreads account so that posts are synchronized there automatically.

Sign up for an Email Marketing Service(EMS) provider. Most have a free tier with all the functions you need to begin. Use the space below to compare different providers. Pricing and functionality matter, and automation is a must.

_____

_____

_____

_____

_____

_____

_____

Include a clear invitation to subscribe to your newsletter. Write phrases to invite readers to subscribe to your newsletter. Be specific about what you offer them. A simple "Let's keep in touch" is not as effective as "Grab your free book now."

_____

_____

_____

_____

_____

_____

_____

_____

_____

_____

_____

_____

_____

_____

_____

_____

_____

_____

You have laid the foundation. GREAT JOB! Now, you can continue with your first monthly tasks.

Dream Big!

Start Small!

Act Now!

Create your calendar. Write down dates and times for events, appointments, meetings, and deadlines.

Month _____/_____

To do list:	M	T	W

T	F	S	S

BUDGET

Month _____/_____

Expense	Planned	Actual

Monthly tasks:

At the end of your book, include an invitation for readers to subscribe to your newsletter. Add a QR code to your physical book and a link at the end of your digital book.

Create and publish your A+ Content. What aspects do you want to highlight in your A+ Content? Would you like to include illustrations from the book or images of children reading?

_____

_____

_____

_____

_____

_____

_____

Create activity sheets or class lessons to accompany your book. Write down ideas for supplemental materials that can serve as lead magnets (what subscribers receive in exchange for joining your email list). Suggestions:

_____

_____

_____

_____

_____

_____

_____

Consider creating a Book Funnel account (optional) – a great way to deliver files to your subscribers.

<u>Book Funnel Promos:</u>

Newsletters Promos are for building an email list. You can participate with a book, an excerpt, or activity sheets.

Newsletter Promos: _____
Dates Running: _____
Dates you share: _____
Platforms you share on: _____
_____
_____
Number of participants _____
Subscribers gained _____

Newsletter Promos: _____
Dates Running: _____
Dates you share: _____
Platforms you share on: _____
_____
_____
Number of participants _____
Subscribers gained _____

Newsletter Promos: _____
Dates Running: _____
Dates you share: _____
Platforms you share on: _____
_____
_____
Number of participants _____
Subscribers gained _____

Sales Promos are for bringing attention to your Amazon listing.

Sales Promos: _____

Dates Running: _____

Dates you share: _____

Platforms you share on: _____

_____

Number of participants _____

Sales _____

Sales Promos: _____

Dates Running: _____

Dates you share: _____

Platforms you share on: _____

_____

Number of participants _____

Sales _____

Sales Promos: _____

Dates Running: _____

Dates you share: _____

Platforms you share on: _____

_____

Number of participants _____

Sales _____

Book Funnel is a great way to jumpstart your email list. The platform also gives the option to do author swaps. That means an author writing in your genre sends your book to their email subscribers, and you reciprocate by introducing them to your subscribers.

Set up your email automation.

Here are a few ideas for an automated email sequence:
Welcome to My Story World! Here's a Special Gift for You
The Story Behind [Book Title]
How to help your kids fall in love with books
Meet [Character Name]: Your New Favorite Adventure Buddy
Fun facts I learned about [the subject of your book]
Behind the Pages: A Sneak Peek into My Writing Process
Let's Play! Fun Activities from [Book Title]
Your Questions Answered: All About [Book Title]
What Readers Are Saying: [Book Title] Reviews and Stories
Thank You for Being Part of My Journey – A Special Offer
Inside

Create a list of subject lines related to your book.
Aim for 5–7 emails for your welcome automation drip
campaign.

_____

_____

_____

_____

_____

_____

_____

_____

_____

_____

_____

Create and schedule your social media posts for the month:
If you need inspiration for your posts, download the 35
Social Media Post Ideas from
https://www.dedonibooks.com/resources
Aim for 1-3 a day, 3-7 days a week. Consistency matters.
Vary different formats:
Meet character - graphic
My writing space/ritual – picture
Flip through a book – reel

Date Scheduled/Subject/ Platform
Format type and other notes.

01/01/2025 / Happy New Year/ Reel with fireworks/ IG
A picture of kids looking at fireworks

_____

_____

_____

_____

_____

_____

_____

_____

_____

_____

_____

_____

_____

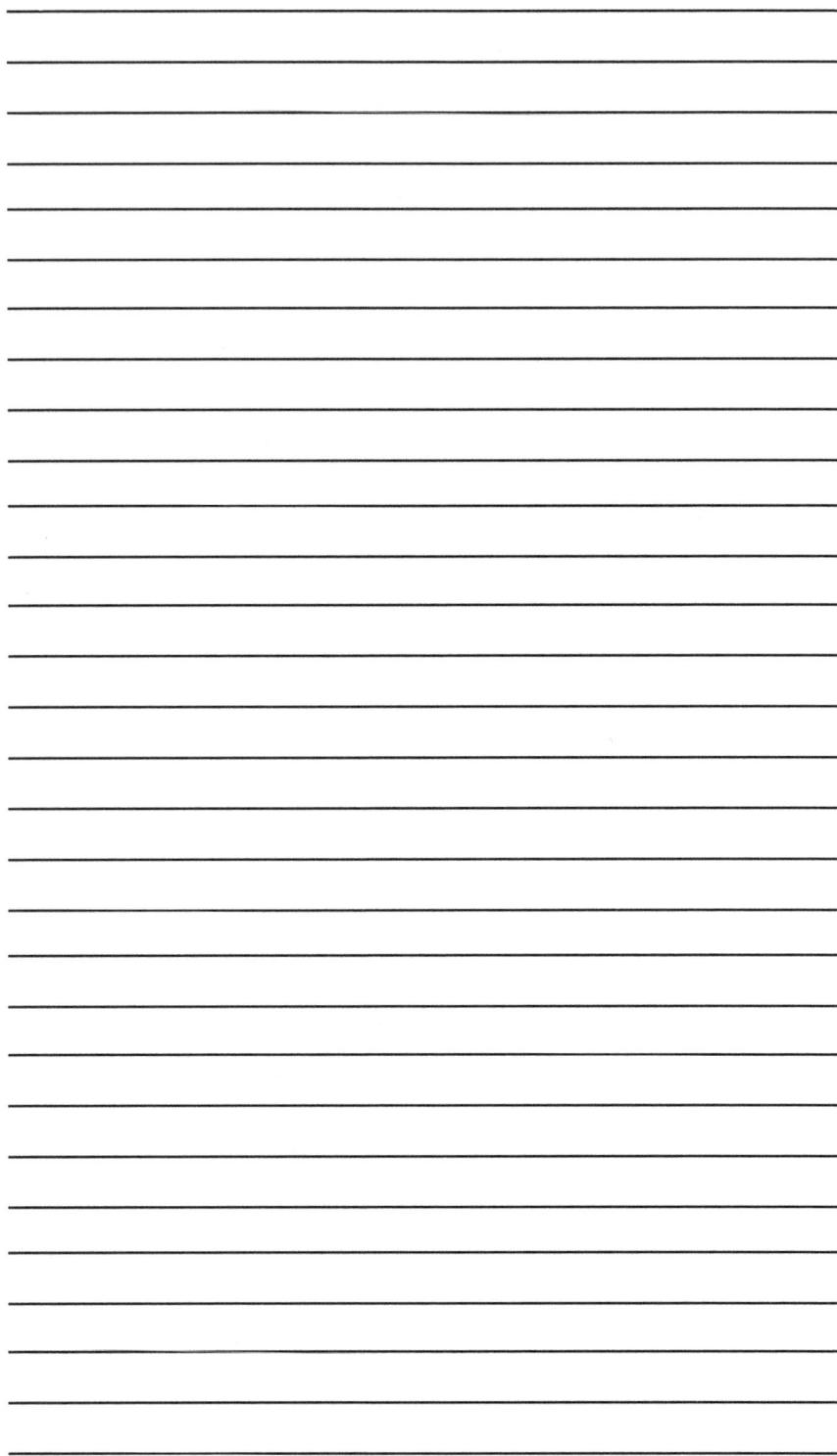

Highlight the content with the most engagement.

Set up your Amazon Ads.
Begin with four ads — automatic, Product, Keyword, and Categories. **Analyze and adjust every two weeks!**

Write down the profitable keywords/phrases after the first two weeks:

_____

_____

_____

_____

_____

_____

_____

_____

_____

_____

_____

Profitable targeted products after first two weeks:

_____

_____

_____

_____

_____

_____

_____

_____

_____

Profitable categories after first two weeks:

_____

_____

_____

_____

_____

_____

Check the search terms of your auto ads and write down the profitable keywords and products. Set up new ads with those.

_____

_____

_____

_____

_____

_____

_____

_____

_____

_____

_____

_____

_____

_____

_____

_____

Brainstorm blog post ideas. Write down your blog post for the month. Title of blog posts:

_____

_____

_____

_____

_____

_____

_____

_____

Newsletter ideas:

_____

_____

_____

_____

_____

_____

_____

_____

_____

_____

_____

_____

_____

You can always reuse the newsletters as blog posts or social media posts.

Biggest accomplishment this month:	Next goal:
What turned out better than expected?	What needs improvement?
New things to try:	Task to focus on:

Use this space to jot down ideas, reminders, and reflections as you work through your tasks. You can even make your own to-do list.

Do not be afraid of growing slowly;
be afraid only of standing still.

Traditional Chinese Proverb

Month _____/_____

To do list:	M	T	W

T	F	S	S

BUDGET

Month _____/_____

Expense	Planned	Actual

Monthly tasks:

Engage with your followers by replying to comments and messages. Also, engage with at least five other accounts by commenting on their posts or sharing their content.

Identify your top competitors in the children's book market. Examine their marketing tactics, such as social media, advertisements, and content strategies. Evaluate their book covers, blurbs, and premium content for inspiration.

Write down the authors and books you admire and what distinguishes them from others.

_____

_____

_____

_____

_____

_____

_____

_____

_____

_____

_____

_____

_____

_____

What can you learn from them?

_____

_____

_____

_____

_____

_____

_____

_____

Identify social media accounts similar to yours. Analyze their performance and most successful posts. What type of posts are most popular? Study how your competitors engage their audience. Identify content types (videos, blogs, images) that perform well for them.

_____

_____

_____

_____

_____

_____

_____

_____

_____

Create a plan to incorporate similar strategies into your
content calendar.

_____

_____

_____

_____

_____

_____

_____

Create and schedule your social media posts for the month:

_____

_____

_____

_____

_____

_____

_____

_____

_____

_____

_____

_____

_____

_____

_____

_____

_____

Highlight the content with the most engagement.

Newsletter ideas:

_____

_____

_____

_____

_____

_____

_____

_____

_____

_____

_____

_____

Test different subject lines and email content to see what converts better. Track results.

_____

_____

_____

_____

_____

_____

_____

_____

_____

Adjust your Amazon Ads.

Profitable keywords:

_____

_____

_____

_____

_____

_____

_____

_____

_____

_____

_____

Profitable targeted products:

_____

_____

_____

_____

_____

_____

_____

_____

_____

_____

_____

_____

Profitable categories:

_____

_____

_____

_____

_____

_____

Check the search terms of your auto ads and write down
the profitable keywords and products. Set up new ads with
those.

_____

_____

_____

_____

_____

_____

_____

_____

_____

_____

_____

Turn off keywords, categories, and products that are
bleeding you money.
Add losing search terms to negative targeting.
Adjust every two weeks.

Schedule Free Kindle Days Promo(s)

Book: Free Kindle Dates:

_____   _____

To maximize exposure, use promo sites like The Fussy
Librarian, Free Booksy, BookBub, and The eReader Cafe. For
best results, spread the promo sites over the duration of
the promo instead of scheduling all on the same day.
Amazon gives more exposure to products that are
consistently on demand vs short term, like a single day.

Paid Promo Sites/Dates/Downloads
_____ /_____ /_____
_____ /_____ /_____
_____ /_____ /_____
_____ /_____ /_____
_____ /_____ /_____

If you have more than one book:

Book: Free Kindle Dates:

_____   _____

Paid Promo Sites/Dates/Downloads
_____ /_____ /_____
_____ /_____ /_____
_____ /_____ /_____
_____ /_____ /_____
_____ /_____ /_____

Always track performance.

Check your recent reviews. What are readers saying about your book(s)? Check other similar books for phrases you can use in your blurb.

_____

_____

_____

_____

_____

_____

_____

_____

_____

_____

_____

_____

_____

_____

_____

_____

_____

_____

_____

_____

_____

_____

_____

Once you have the above information, rewrite your book blurb to target your readers more effectively. If buyers share that your book helps their children overcome a fear, include that in your blurb. If readers say that your book helps their kids make friends at a new school, be sure to mention it in your blurb.

_____

_____

_____

_____

_____

_____

_____

_____

_____

_____

_____

_____

Brainstorm blog post ideas (optional). Write down your blog post for the month. You can always repurpose some of your social media posts or newsletters.

_____

_____

_____

_____

Biggest accomplishment this month:	Next goal:
What turned out better than expected?	What needs improvement?
New things to try:	Task to focus on:

Use this space to jot down ideas, reminders, and reflections as you work through your tasks.

Consistency is the key to success.

Month _____/_____

To do list:	M	T	W

T	F	S	S

BUDGET

Month _____/_____

Expense	Planned	Actual

Monthly tasks:

Set up Google Analytics to track website traffic and user behavior.

Pitch to Local Media: Send press releases or pitch stories to local newspapers, radio stations, or TV shows about your book and any events. Research the editor in charge of the section that aligns with your theme or message.

_____

_____

_____

_____

_____

_____

_____

Compile customer reviews, stories, or testimonials that can be used in your marketing materials.

_____

_____

_____

_____

_____

_____

_____

_____

Review past blog posts and social media content for evergreen material. Repurpose an old blog post into a new video or newsletter. Recycle content by translating it into different formats. Content to repurpose:

_____

_____

_____

_____

_____

_____

Create and schedule your social media posts for the month:

_____

_____

_____

_____

_____

_____

_____

_____

_____

_____

_____

_____

_____

_____

_____

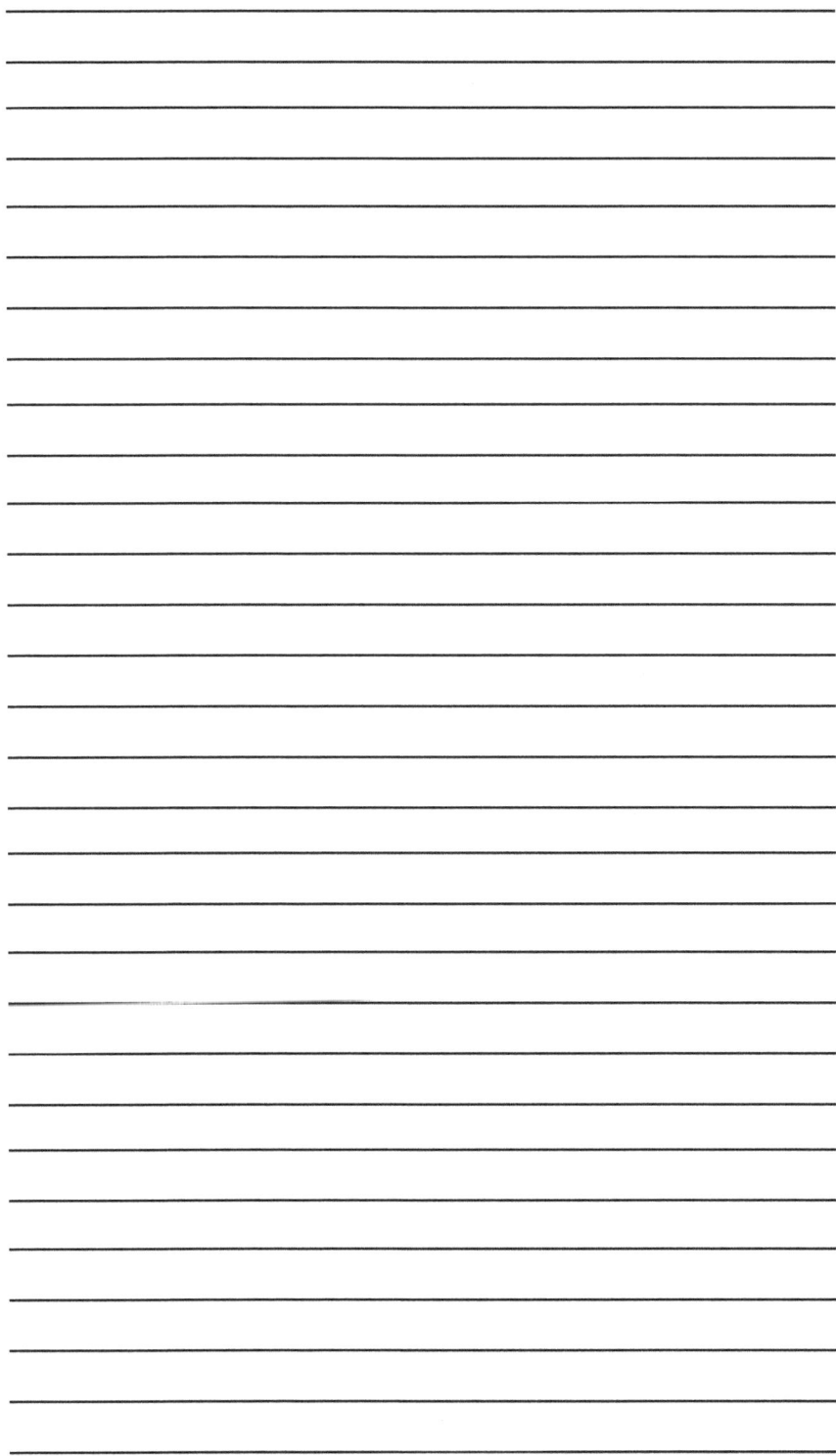

_____

_____

_____

_____

_____

_____

_____

_____

_____

_____

_____

_____

_____

_____

_____

_____

_____

_____

_____

_____

_____

_____

_____

_____

Highlight the content with the most engagement.

Don't forget to engage! Reply to comments on your post. Comment and like posts by others!

Adjust your Amazon Ads.

Profitable keywords:

_____

_____

_____

_____

_____

_____

_____

_____

_____

_____

Profitable targeted products:

_____

_____

_____

_____

_____

_____

_____

_____

_____

_____

Profitable categories:

_____

_____

_____

_____

_____

_____

Check the search terms of your auto ads and write down the profitable keywords and products. Set up new ads with those.

_____

_____

_____

_____

_____

_____

_____

_____

_____

_____

_____

_____

_____

_____

_____

Boost your most successful posts to increase your following. Record the number of profile visits and followers gained:

_____

_____

_____

_____

_____

Track the success of your freebies in growing your email list or engagement. Analyze the success of your email campaigns. Write down the subject lines with the highest open rate:

_____

_____

_____

_____

_____

_____

_____

Create and schedule your monthly newsletters using the information you gained from your analyses. Subject lines used:

_____

_____

_____

_____

_____

Blog posts for the month:

_____

_____

_____

_____

_____

_____

_____

Draft an email to propose a collaboration with influencers and bloggers. Write down ideas why your book might be good for their feeds, but don't forget to personalize each email.

_____

_____

_____

_____

_____

_____

_____

_____

_____

_____

_____

_____

_____

_____

Identify Influencers and bloggers and send emails asking to collaborate. Record the answers and materials sent.

Influencers/reach (#of followers) / email sent date/
Keep track of answers, books sent, dates of posts or blogs going live, and results like a bump in sales or followers.

_____/_____ /_____
_____
_____

_____/_____ /_____
_____
_____

_____/_____ /_____
_____
_____

_____/_____ /_____
_____
_____

_____/_____ /_____
_____
_____

_____/_____ /_____
_____
_____

_____/_____ /_____
_____
_____

_____/_____ /_____
_____
_____

_____/_____ /_____
_____
_____

_____/_____ /_____
_____
_____

_____/_____ /_____
_____
_____

_____/_____ /_____
_____
_____

_____/_____ /_____
_____
_____

_____/_____ /_____
_____
_____

_____/_____ /_____
_____
_____

Always do your best to track results.

Biggest accomplishment this month:	Next goal:
What turned out better than expected?	What needs improvement?
New things to try:	Task to focus on:

Use this space to jot down ideas, reminders, and reflections as you work through your tasks.

Every action gets you closer to your goal.

Month _____/_____

To do list:	M	T	W

T	F	S	S

BUDGET

Month _____/_____

Expense	Planned	Actual

Monthly tasks:

Check your website analytics. Works on SEO. Each page needs to have a name and a relevant description. Make sure the images on your website have short descriptions. Double-check that each link leads to its intended destination.

Engage with your followers by replying to comments and messages. Also, engage with at least five other accounts by commenting on their posts or sharing their content.

Analyze your social media activity, including what worked and what didn't.

Most successful post for the month:

_____
_____
_____
_____
_____
_____
_____

What appeals to your followers?

_____
_____
_____
_____
_____
_____

What doesn't get enough engagement?

_____

_____

_____

_____

_____

_____

_____

Create and schedule Social Media posts based on the above analysis.

_____

_____

_____

_____

_____

_____

_____

_____

_____

_____

_____

_____

_____

_____

_____

_____

_____

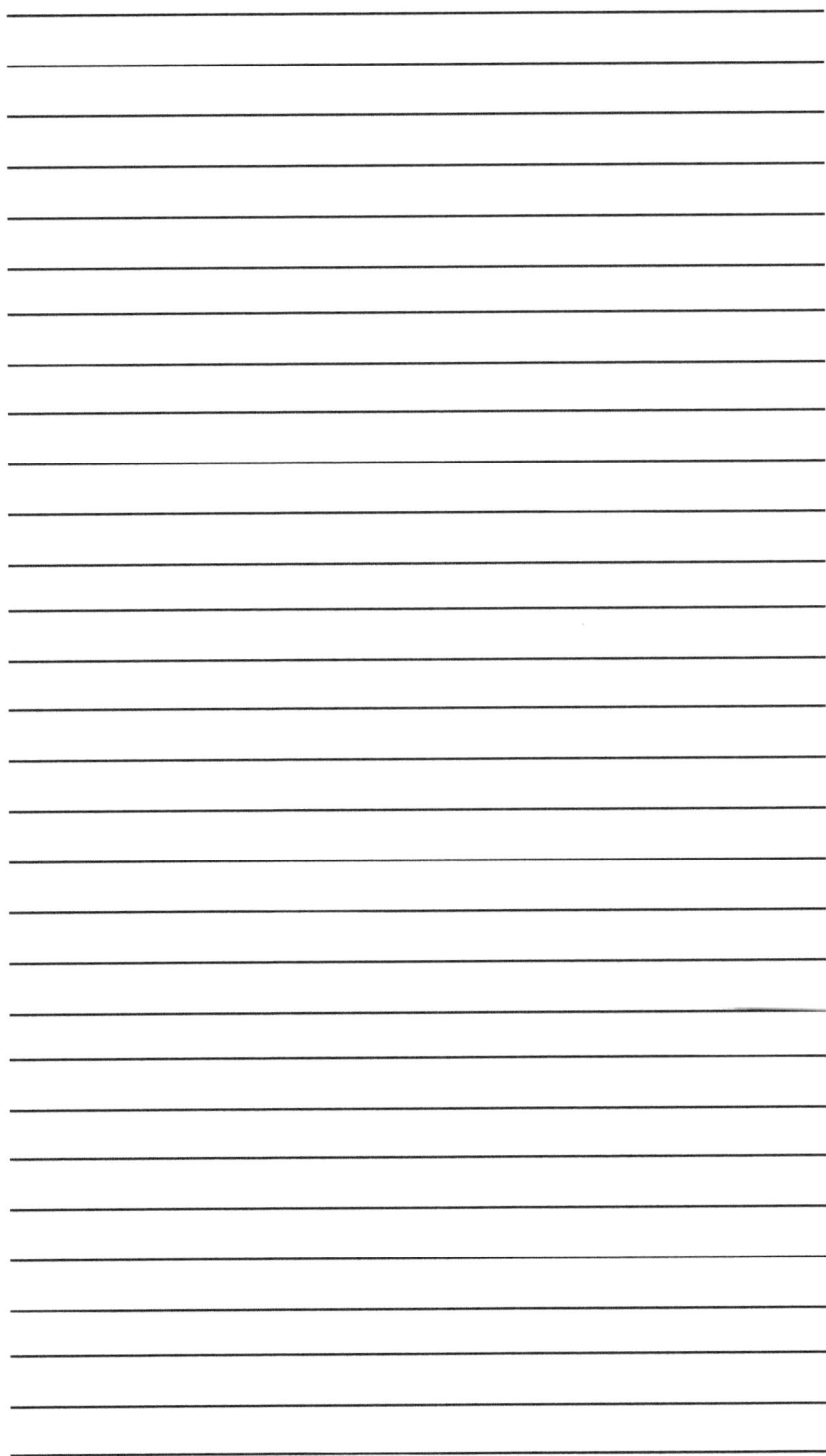

_____

_____

_____

_____

_____

_____

_____

_____

_____

_____

_____

_____

_____

_____

_____

_____

_____

_____

_____

_____

_____

_____

_____

_____

_____

_____

_____

Highlight the content with the most engagement.

Adjust your Amazon Ads.

Profitable keywords:

_____

_____

_____

_____

_____

_____

_____

_____

_____

_____

Profitable targeted products:

_____

_____

_____

_____

_____

_____

_____

_____

_____

_____

_____

Profitable categories:

_____

_____

_____

_____

_____

_____

Check the search terms of your auto ads and write down the profitable keywords and products. Set up new ads with those.

_____

_____

_____

_____

_____

_____

_____

_____

_____

_____

_____

_____

_____

_____

_____

Explore using Sponsored Brands or Sponsored Display ads.

_____

_____

_____

_____

_____

Collect and analyze recent reviews from Amazon, Goodreads, and other platforms. Write down comments and phrases you can use in your marketing campaign.

_____

_____

_____

_____

_____

_____

_____

_____

_____

_____

_____

_____

_____

_____

_____

_____

Research trending topics in children's literature and incorporate them into your blog and social media posts.

_____

_____

_____

_____

_____

_____

_____

_____

_____

_____

_____

_____

_____

_____

_____

_____

_____

_____

_____

_____

_____

_____

_____

_____

_____

_____

Newsletter ideas:

_____

_____

_____

_____

_____

_____

_____

_____

_____

Test different subject lines and email content to see what converts better. Track results.

_____

_____

_____

_____

_____

_____

_____

_____

_____

_____

_____

Pitch your book to reading blogs or YouTube channels.

YouTube Channel /# of subscribers/email sent date/
answer/results (views and comments)

_____/_____ /_____
_____

_____/_____ /_____
_____

_____/_____ /_____
_____

_____/_____ /_____
_____

_____/_____ /_____
_____

_____/_____ /_____
_____

_____/_____ /_____
_____

_____/_____ /_____
_____

_____/_____ /_____
_____

_____/_____ /_____
_____

Biggest accomplishment this month:	Next goal:
What turned out better than expected?	What needs improvement?
New things to try:	Task to focus on:

Use this space to jot down ideas, reminders, and reflections as you work through your tasks.

What you
do today
defines your
tomorrow.

Month _____/_____

To do list:	M	T	W

T	F	S	S

BUDGET

Month _____/_____

Expense	Planned	Actual

Monthly tasks:

Update your website and social media with testimonials from satisfied readers.

Engage with your followers by replying to comments and messages. Also, engage with at least five other accounts by commenting on their posts or sharing their content.

Review the competition's ads for ideas and inspiration. Facebook (Meta) Ad Library is a public resource that gives you access to competitors' ads.
https://www.facebook.com/ads/library/
Write down ideas and inspirations:

_____

_____

_____

_____

_____

_____

_____

_____

_____

_____

_____

_____

_____

_____

Create and schedule your social media posts for the month:

_____

_____

_____

_____

_____

_____

_____

_____

_____

_____

_____

_____

_____

_____

_____

_____

_____

_____

_____

_____

_____

_____

_____

_____

_____

_____

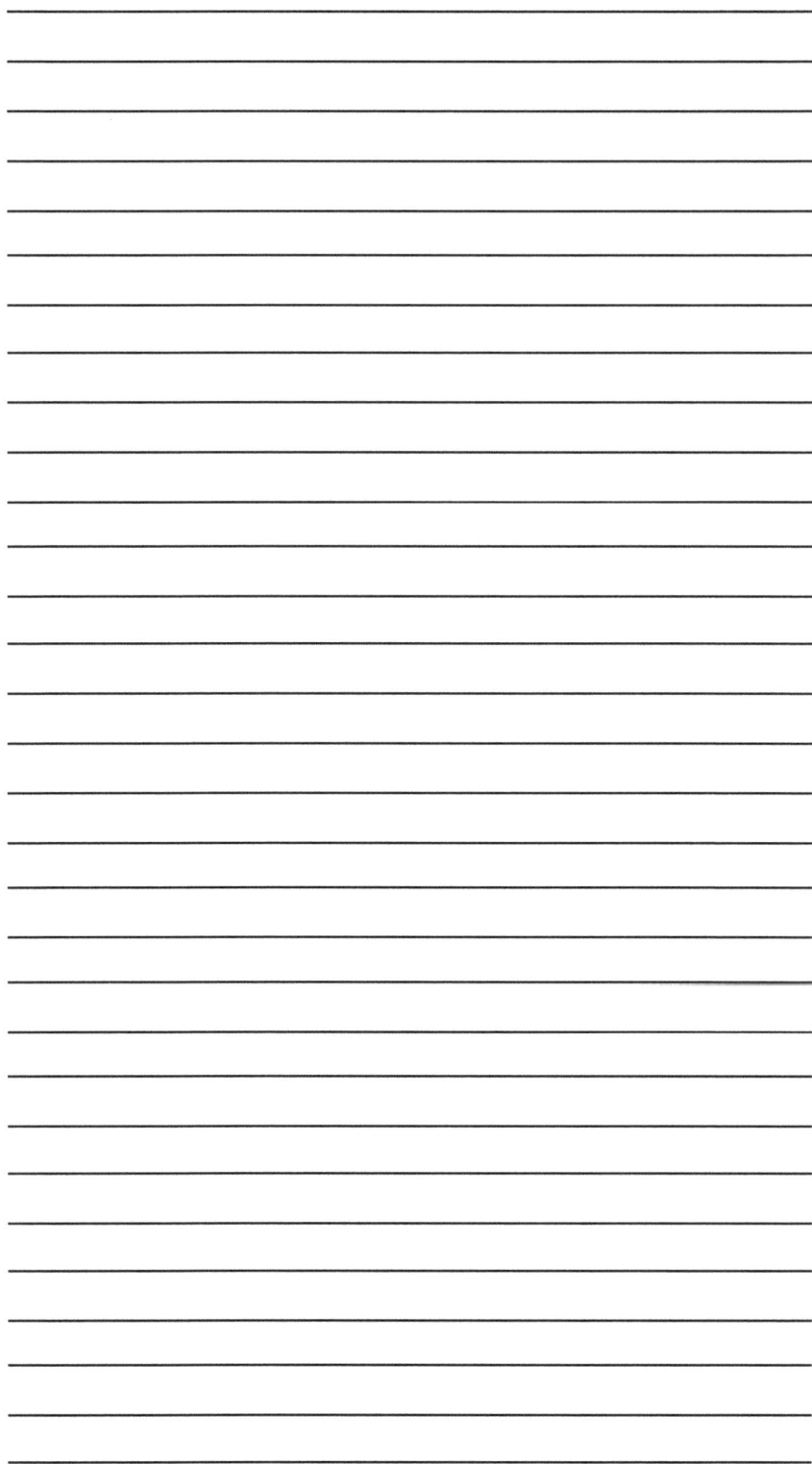

Adjust your Amazon Ads.

Profitable keywords:

_____

_____

_____

_____

_____

_____

_____

_____

_____

_____

Profitable targeted products:

_____

_____

_____

_____

_____

_____

_____

_____

_____

_____

Profitable categories:

_____

_____

_____

_____

_____

Other Profitable ads:

_____

_____

_____

_____

Check the search terms of your auto ads and write down
the profitable keywords and products. Set up new ads with
those.

_____

_____

_____

_____

_____

_____

_____

_____

Newsletter and blog ideas:

_____

_____

_____

_____

_____

_____

_____

_____

_____

_____

_____

_____

_____

_____

_____

_____

_____

_____

_____

_____

_____

_____

_____

_____

_____

_____

Biggest accomplishment this month:	Next goal:
What turned out better than expected?	What needs improvement?
New things to try:	Task to focus on:

Use this space to jot down ideas, reminders, and reflections as you work through your tasks.

Each step forward, no matter how small, is a victory.

Month _____/_____

To do list:	M	T	W

T	F	S	S

BUDGET

Month _____/_____

Expense	Planned	Actual

Monthly tasks:

It's time to update your supplemental materials. Brainstorm ideas for new activity sheets, class lessons, or other resources that can support your book.

_____

_____

_____

_____

_____

Consider video marketing.

Create Book Trailers: Develop engaging videos introducing your book's theme and story. Share these across social media, your website, email campaigns, and Amazon product page (as long as you do not mention Amazon in them).

Author Video Series: Consider starting a video series where you talk about your writing process and character development or read excerpts from your book.

_____

_____

_____

_____

_____

_____

_____

_____

_____

Engage with your followers by replying to comments and messages. Engage with at least five other accounts by commenting on their post or sharing their content.

Identify social media accounts similar to yours. Analyze their performance and most successful posts. What type of posts are most popular?

_____
_____
_____
_____
_____
_____
_____

Brainstorm ideas for how to expand on it or create similar content.

_____
_____
_____
_____
_____
_____
_____
_____
_____
_____
_____

Outline ideas for a series of posts, emails, or blogs. This could include daily introductions of your characters or a step-by-step account of your book creation process.

_____

_____

_____

_____

_____

_____

_____

_____

_____

_____

_____

_____

_____

_____

_____

_____

_____

_____

_____

_____

_____

_____

_____

_____

_____

Create and schedule your social media posts for the month:

_____

_____

_____

_____

_____

_____

_____

_____

_____

_____

_____

_____

_____

_____

_____

_____

_____

_____

_____

_____

_____

_____

_____

_____

_____

_____

_____

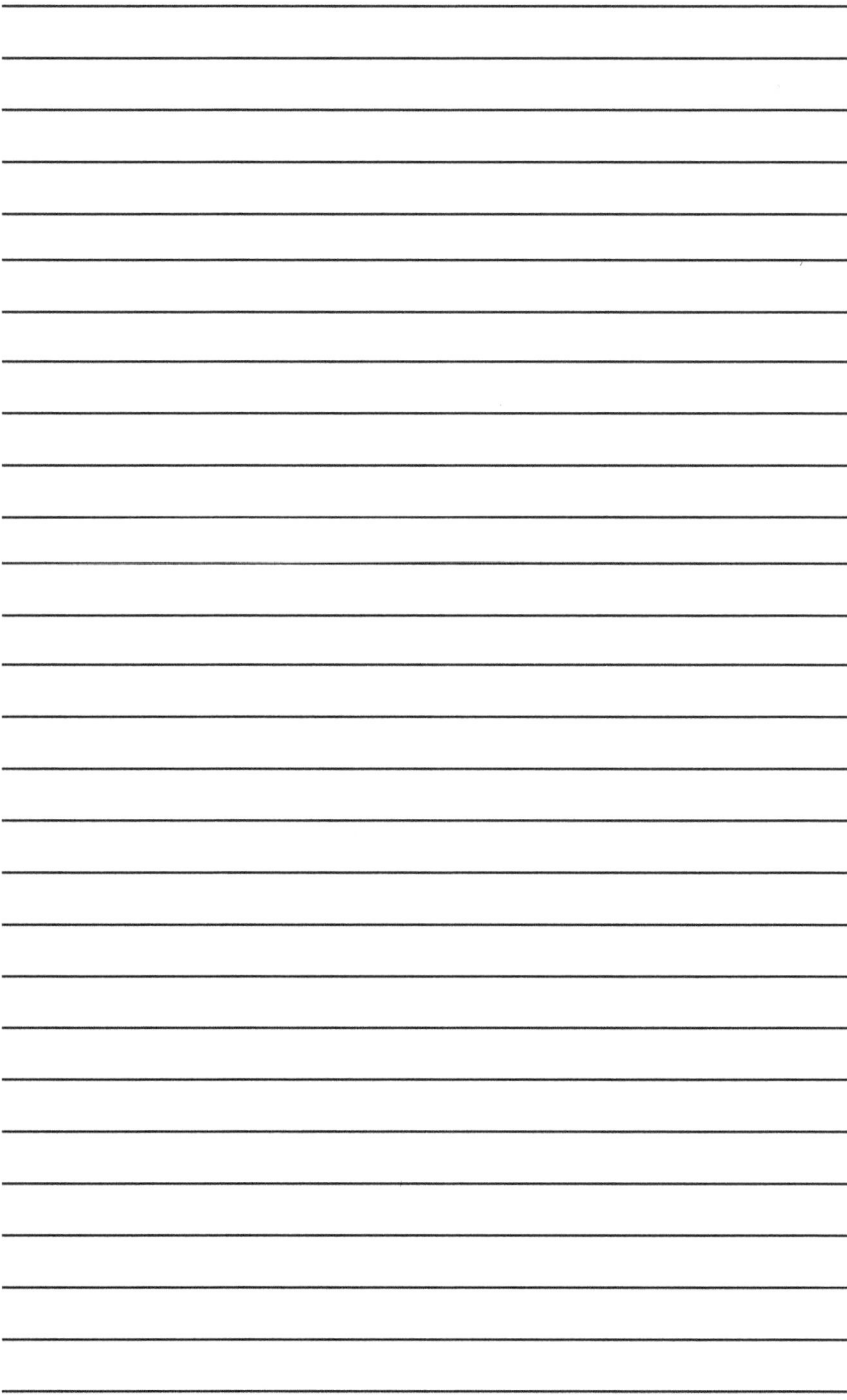

Adjust your Amazon Ads.

Profitable keywords:

_____

_____

_____

_____

_____

_____

_____

_____

_____

_____

Profitable targeted products:

_____

_____

_____

_____

_____

_____

_____

_____

_____

_____

Profitable categories:

_____

_____

_____

_____

_____

_____

Check the search terms of your auto ads and write down the profitable keywords and products. Set up new ads with those.

_____

_____

_____

_____

_____

_____

_____

_____

_____

_____

_____

_____

_____

_____

Track the success of your freebies in growing your email list or engagement. Analyze the success of your email campaigns. Write down the subject lines that have the highest open rates:

_____

_____

_____

_____

_____

_____

_____

Create and schedule your monthly newsletters using the information you gained from your analyses. Subject lines used:

_____

_____

_____

_____

_____

_____

_____

_____

_____

_____

_____

_____

_____

Biggest accomplishment this month:	Next goal:
What turned out better than expected?	What needs improvement?
New things to try:	Task to focus on:

Use this space to jot down ideas, reminders,
and reflections as you work through your tasks.

You are doing amazing!

It has been six months, and by now, you have a pretty good idea of what works and what doesn't.
It's time to update your book description and customer personas with all the insights you've gained so far.
This step is not mandatory but highly recommended.

Title of the book:

Genre and intended age group:

_____

What is your book about? What is the message?

_____
_____
_____
_____
_____
_____
_____

What do others say your book is about?

_____
_____
_____
_____
_____
_____
_____
_____
_____
_____
_____

What problems does your book solve? How does it help readers?

_____

_____

_____

_____

_____

Does your book fit in a niche?

_____

_____

Do your "survey." Study your book's reviews on Amazon and Goodreads. Write down the positive comments and phrases readers say about your book. That will help you craft and improve your blurb.

_____

_____

_____

_____

_____

_____

_____

_____

_____

_____

_____

Find successful books that are similar to yours and read their reviews. That will help you understand what buyers are looking for.

Title:_____ by:_____
Title:_____ by:_____
Title:_____ by:_____
Title:_____ by:_____
Title:_____ by:_____
Title:_____ by:_____
Title:_____ by:_____
Title:_____ by:_____
Title:_____ by:_____
Title:_____ by:_____

Write down positive comments and phrases used in the reviews of those books that can be used in your blurb:

_____
_____
_____
_____
_____
_____
_____
_____
_____
_____
_____
_____
_____

What categories does your book fit in? Write down all categories and pick the best fit. Pick the best three for your book.

_____

_____

_____

_____

_____

_____

_____

_____

_____

_____

KDP Keywords:

_____

_____

_____

_____

_____

_____

_____

_____

_____

_____

_____

Notes:

Do your "survey." Go through your book reviews and write down the positive comments readers share about your book. What do people believe your book is about? What do they appreciate most about it? How does your book benefit them or their children?

_____

_____

_____

_____

_____

_____

_____

_____

What did you learn about your audience?

_____

_____

_____

_____

_____

_____

_____

_____

Customer Persona:

Define your target audience. Give your customer persona a name (parent, teacher, etc.) What is their relationship to the child?

Child's interests:

_____
_____
_____
_____

Child's struggles:

_____
_____
_____

Customer's challenges:

_____
_____
_____

Customer's goals:

_____
_____
_____

Where do they get their recommendations from?

_____

_____

_____

Where do they shop?

_____

_____

_____

Preferred book features:

_____

_____

_____

_____

Other important information about your customer:

_____

_____

_____

_____

_____

_____

_____

_____

_____

Revise your book blurb to better engage your readers.

_____

_____

_____

_____

_____

_____

_____

_____

_____

_____

_____

_____

_____

_____

_____

_____

_____

_____

_____

_____

_____

_____

_____

_____

Use this space to rewrite the blurbs for your other books or to jot down ideas for future improvements.

_____
_____
_____
_____
_____
_____
_____
_____
_____
_____
_____
_____
_____
_____
_____
_____
_____
_____
_____
_____
_____
_____
_____
_____
_____
_____

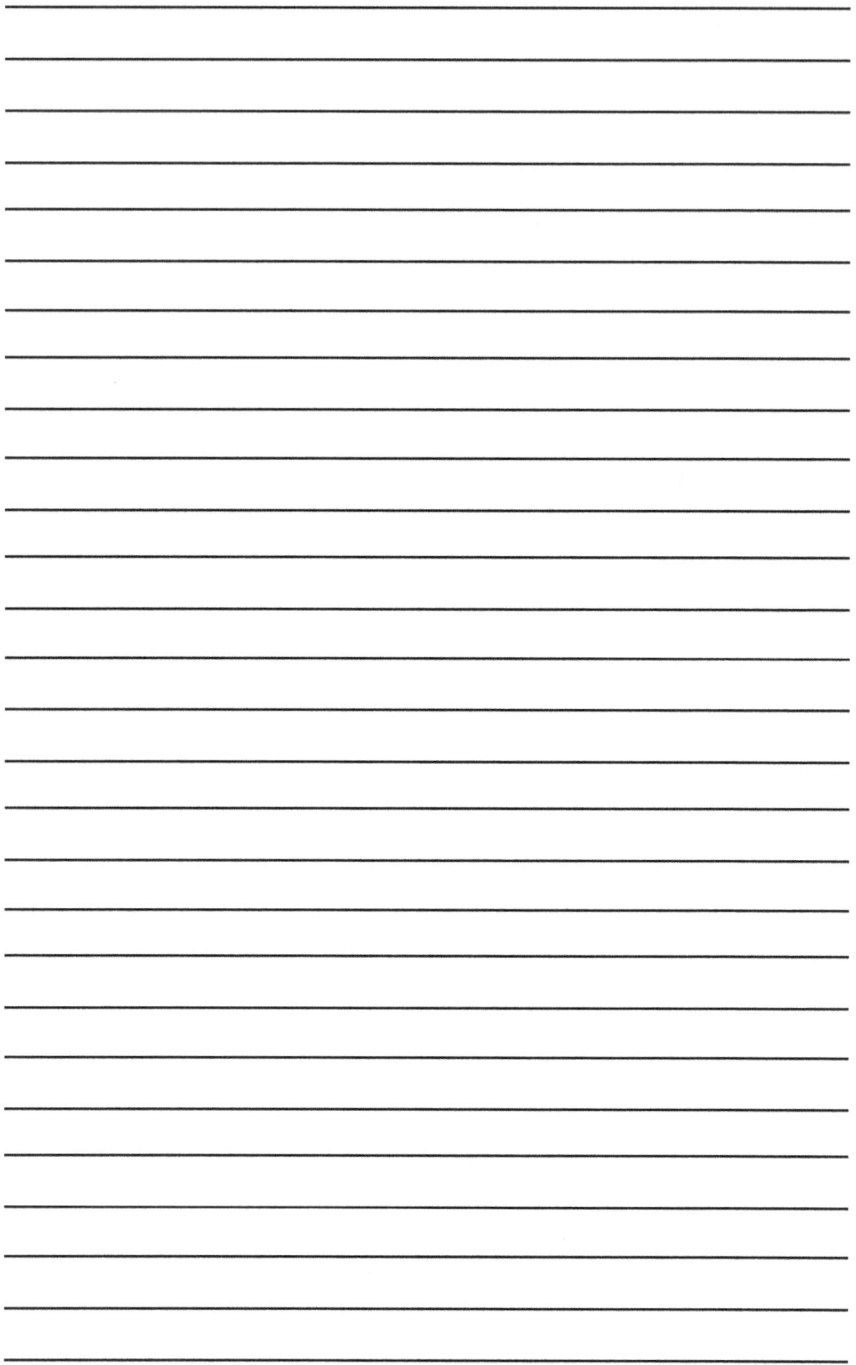

You're on the right path—just keep moving forward.

Month _____/_____

To do list:	M	T	W

T	F	S	S

BUDGET

Month _____ / _____

Expense	Planned	Actual

Tasks for this month:

Update the website with new information, reviews, awards, or news for upcoming books or events, if applicable.

_____

_____

_____

_____

_____

_____

_____

_____

Revise the call to action in your email sign-up form according to your insights so far. New call to action:

_____

_____

_____

_____

_____

_____

_____

_____

_____

_____

_____

_____

Update your activity sheets or class lessons. Write down ideas for new supplemental materials that can serve as lead magnets.

_____

_____

_____

_____

_____

_____

_____

_____

_____

_____

_____

_____

_____

_____

_____

_____

_____

_____

_____

_____

_____

_____

_____

Book Funnel Promos:

Newsletter Promo: _____

Dates Running: _____

Dates you share: _____

Platforms you share on: _____

_____

_____

Number of participants _____

Subscribers gained _____

Newsletter Promo: _____

Dates Running: _____

Dates you share: _____

Platforms you share on: _____

_____

_____

Number of participants _____

Subscribers gained _____

Newsletter Promo: _____

Dates Running: _____

Dates you share: _____

Platforms you share on: _____

_____

_____

Number of participants _____

Subscribers gained _____

Sales Promo: _____

Dates Running: _____

Dates you share: _____

Platforms you share on: _____

_____

Number of participants _____

Sales _____

Sales Promos: _____

Dates Running: _____

Dates you share: _____

Platforms you share on: _____

_____

Number of participants _____

Sales _____

Sales Promos: _____

Dates Running: _____

Dates you share: _____

Platforms you share on: _____

_____

Number of participants _____

Sales _____

Update your email automation if needed.

What email subject lines have the highest open rate so far?

_____

_____

_____

_____

_____

Write down some new subject lines pertaining to you or
your book.

_____

_____

_____

_____

_____

_____

_____

_____

Plan your monthly newsletters:

_____

_____

_____

_____

_____

Create and schedule your social media posts for the month:

_____

_____

_____

_____

_____

_____

_____

_____

_____

_____

_____

_____

_____

_____

_____

_____

_____

_____

_____

_____

_____

_____

_____

_____

_____

_____

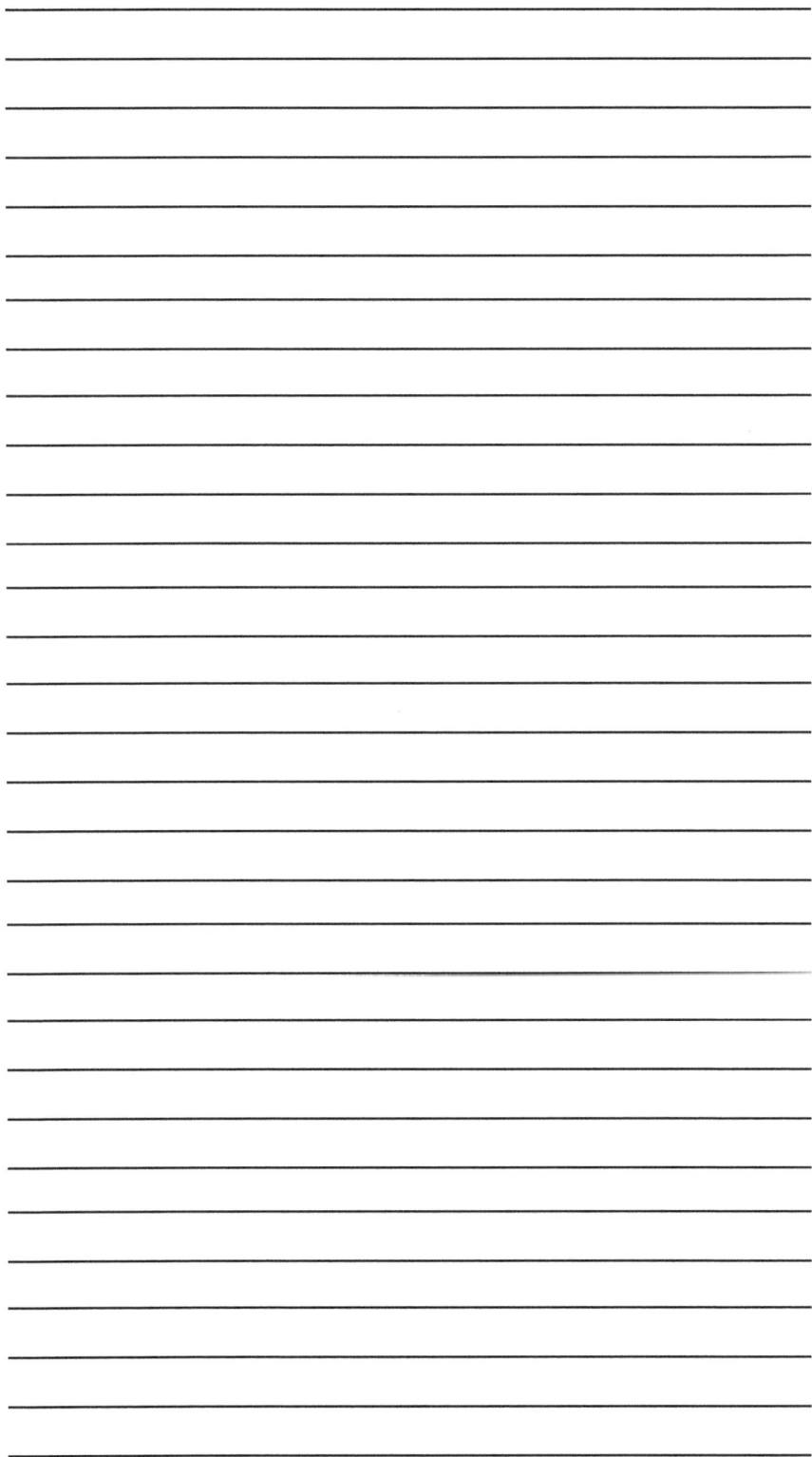

Adjust your Amazon Ads.

Profitable keywords/phrases:

_____

_____

_____

_____

_____

_____

_____

_____

_____

_____

Profitable targeted products:

_____

_____

_____

_____

_____

_____

_____

_____

_____

_____

Profitable categories:

_____

_____

_____

_____

_____

Check the search terms of your auto ads and write down the profitable keywords and products. Set up new ads with those.

_____

_____

_____

_____

_____

_____

_____

_____

_____

_____

_____

_____

_____

_____

Brainstorm blog post ideas (optional.) Write down your blog post for the month. Title of blog posts:

_____

_____

_____

_____

_____

_____

_____

_____

_____

_____

Update your A+ Content. What do you want to stress about in your A+ Content?

_____

_____

_____

_____

_____

_____

_____

_____

_____

_____

_____

_____

Biggest accomplishment this month:	Next goal:
What turned out better than expected?	What needs improvement?
New things to try:	Task to focus on:

Use this space to jot down ideas, reminders,
and reflections as you work through your tasks.

"*Success usually comes to those who are too busy to be looking for it.*"

Henry David Thoreau

Month _____/_____

To do list:	M	T	W

T	F	S	S

BUDGET

Month _____/_____

Expense	Planned	Actual

Monthly tasks:

Engage with your followers by replying to comments and messages. Engage with at least five other accounts by commenting on their post or sharing their content.

Follow up on top competitors in the children's book market. Analyze their marketing strategies, including social media, ads, and content. Review their book covers, blurbs, and A+ content for ideas.

Authors and books you admire:

_____

_____

_____

_____

_____

_____

_____

_____

_____

_____

_____

_____

_____

_____

_____

_____

_____

What can you learn from them?

_____

_____

_____

_____

_____

_____

_____

_____

_____

_____

_____

_____

_____

_____

_____

_____

_____

_____

_____

_____

_____

_____

_____

_____

_____

_____

Identify social media accounts similar to yours. Analyze their performance and most successful posts. What type of posts are most popular? Study how your competitors engage their audience. Identify content types (videos, blogs, images) that perform well for them.

_____
_____
_____
_____
_____
_____
_____
_____
_____
_____
_____
_____
_____
_____
_____
_____
_____
_____
_____
_____
_____
_____
_____

Create a plan to incorporate similar strategies into your content calendar and email marketing.

_____

_____

_____

_____

_____

_____

_____

_____

_____

_____

_____

_____

_____

_____

_____

_____

_____

_____

_____

_____

_____

_____

_____

_____

_____

Create and schedule your social media posts for the month:

_____

_____

_____

_____

_____

_____

_____

_____

_____

_____

_____

_____

_____

_____

_____

_____

_____

_____

_____

_____

_____

_____

_____

_____

_____

_____

_____

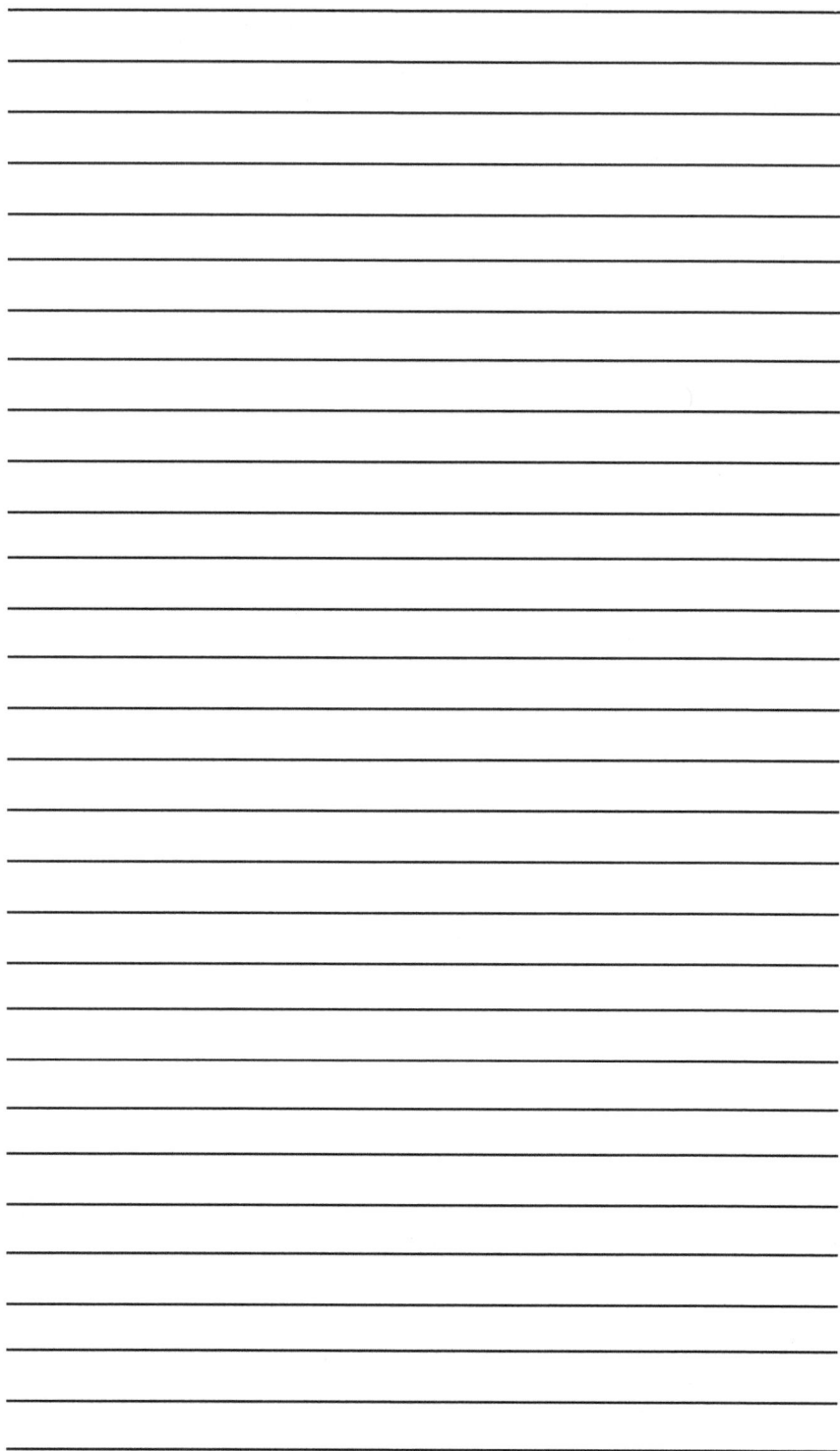

Adjust your Amazon Ads.

Profitable keywords:

_____
_____
_____
_____
_____
_____
_____
_____
_____
_____
_____

Profitable targeted products:

_____
_____
_____
_____
_____
_____
_____
_____
_____

Profitable categories:

_____

_____

_____

_____

_____

Check the search terms of your auto ads and write down
the profitable keywords and products. Set up new ads with
those.

_____

_____

_____

_____

_____

_____

_____

_____

_____

_____

_____

_____

_____

Schedule Free Kindle Days Promo(s)

Book: Free Kindle Dates:

_____   _____

To maximize exposure, combine with promo sites like The Fussy Librarian, Free Booksy, BookBub, and The eReader Cafe. For best result schedule spread the promo sites over the duration of the promo instead of scheduling all on the same day.

Paid Promo Sites/Dates/Downloads
_____ /_____ /_____
_____ /_____ /_____
_____ /_____ /_____
_____ /_____ /_____
_____ /_____ /_____

If you have more than one book:

Book: Free Kindle Dates:

_____   _____

Paid Promo Sites/Dates/Downloads
_____ /_____ /_____
_____ /_____ /_____
_____ /_____ /_____
_____ /_____ /_____
_____ /_____ /_____

Always track performance.

Check your recent reviews. What are readers saying about your book(s)?

_____

_____

_____

_____

_____

_____

_____

_____

After gathering the information above, revise your book blurb to better target your readers.

_____

_____

_____

_____

_____

_____

_____

_____

_____

_____

_____

_____

_____

Biggest accomplishment this month:	Next goal:
What turned out better than expected?	What needs improvement?
New things to try:	Task to focus on:

Use this space to jot down ideas, reminders, and reflections as you work through your tasks.

Keep going!
You're closer
than you think.

Month _____/_____

To do list:	M	T	W

T	F	S	S

BUDGET

Month _____/_____

Expense	Planned	Actual

Monthly tasks:

Gather customer reviews and testimonials that can be utilized in your marketing materials.

Review previous blog posts and social media content for evergreen material. Transform an old blog post into a new video or newsletter. repurpose content by converting it into different formats. Content to recycle:

_____

_____

_____

_____

_____

_____

_____

_____

_____

_____

_____

_____

_____

_____

_____

_____

Don't forget to engage! Reply to comments on your post. Comment and like posts by others!

Create and schedule your social media posts for the month:

_____

_____

_____

_____

_____

_____

_____

_____

_____

_____

_____

_____

_____

_____

_____

_____

_____

_____

_____

_____

_____

_____

_____

_____

_____

_____

_____

_____

_____

_____

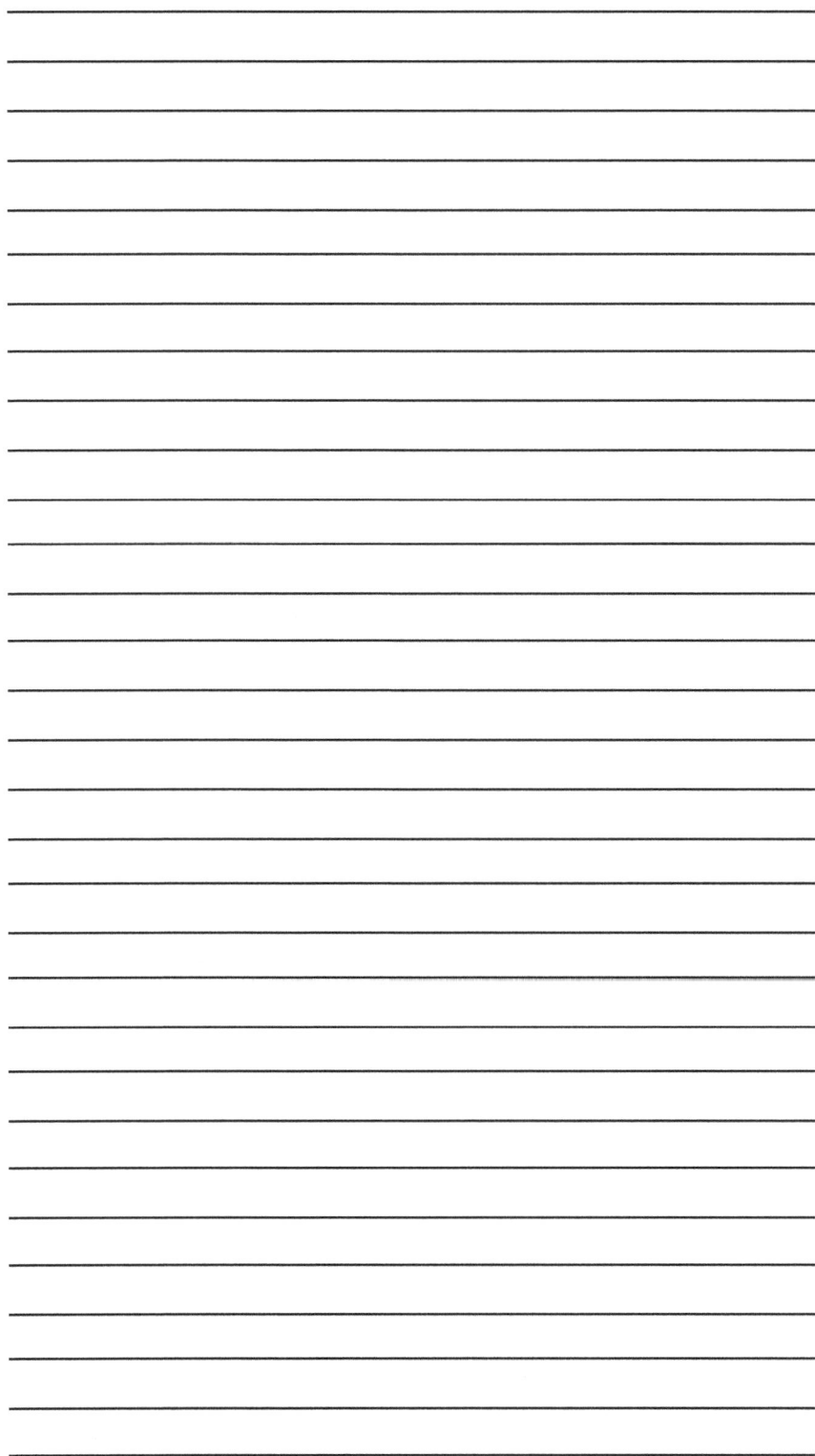

Boost your most successful social media posts to increase your following. Record the number of profile visits and followers gained:

_____

_____

_____

_____

_____

Track the success of your freebies in growing your email list or engagement. Analyze the success of your email campaigns. Write down the subject lines with the highest open rate:

_____

_____

_____

_____

_____

_____

_____

_____

_____

_____

_____

_____

_____

_____

_____

Adjust your Amazon Ads.

Profitable keywords:

_____

_____

_____

_____

_____

_____

_____

_____

_____

_____

_____

Profitable targeted products:

_____

_____

_____

_____

_____

_____

_____

_____

_____

_____

_____

_____

Profitable categories:

_____

_____

_____

_____

_____

_____

Check the search terms of your auto ads and write down the profitable keywords and products. Set up new ads with those.

_____

_____

_____

_____

_____

_____

_____

_____

_____

_____

_____

_____

_____

_____

_____

Create and schedule your monthly newsletters using the information you gained from your analyses. Subject lines used:

_____

_____

_____

_____

_____

_____

_____

_____

Newsletters or blog posts for the month:

_____

_____

_____

_____

_____

_____

_____

_____

_____

_____

_____

_____

Draft an email to propose a collaboration with influencers and bloggers. Write down ideas why your book might be good for their feeds, but don't forget to personalize each email.

_____

_____

_____

_____

_____

_____

_____

_____

_____

_____

_____

_____

_____

_____

_____

_____

_____

_____

_____

_____

_____

_____

Identify Influencers and bloggers and send emails asking to collaborate. Record answer and material sent.

Influencers / reach (#of followers) / email sent date/ Keep track of answers, book sent, dates of post or blog goes live, and results like a bump in sales or followers.

_____/_____ /_____
_____
_____

_____/_____ /_____
_____
_____

_____/_____ /_____
_____
_____

_____/_____ /_____
_____
_____

_____/_____ /_____
_____
_____

_____/_____ /_____
_____
_____

_____/_____/_____
_____
_____

_____/_____/_____
_____
_____

_____/_____/_____
_____
_____

_____/_____/_____
_____
_____

_____/_____/_____
_____
_____

_____/_____/_____
_____
_____

_____/_____/_____
_____
_____

Always do your best to track results.

Biggest accomplishment this month:	*Next goal:*
What turned out better than expected?	*What needs improvement?*
New things to try:	*Task to focus on:*

Use this space to jot down ideas, reminders, and reflections as you work through your tasks.

You're making amazing progress— believe in yourself!

Month _____/_____

To do list:	M	T	W

T	F	S	S

BUDGET

Month _____/_____

Expense	Planned	Actual

Monthly tasks:

Check your website analytics. Focus on SEO. Each page should have a title and a relevant description. Ensure that the images on your website also have a brief description. Double-check that each link leads to its intended destination.

Interact with your followers by responding to comments and messages. Additionally, connect with at least five other accounts by commenting on their posts or sharing their content.

Review your social media activity, noting what was effective and what wasn't.

Most successful post for the month:

_____

_____

_____

_____

_____

_____

_____

_____

_____

_____

_____

Brainstorm ideas for how to expand on it or create similar content.

_____

_____

_____

_____

_____

_____

_____

_____

_____

_____

_____

_____

_____

_____

Boost your most successful posts to increase your following. Record the number of profile visits and followers gained:

_____

_____

_____

_____

_____

What type of posts didn't do well:

_____

_____

_____

_____

_____

_____

_____

Create and schedule Social Media posts based on the above analysis.

_____

_____

_____

_____

_____

_____

_____

_____

_____

_____

_____

_____

_____

_____

_____

_____

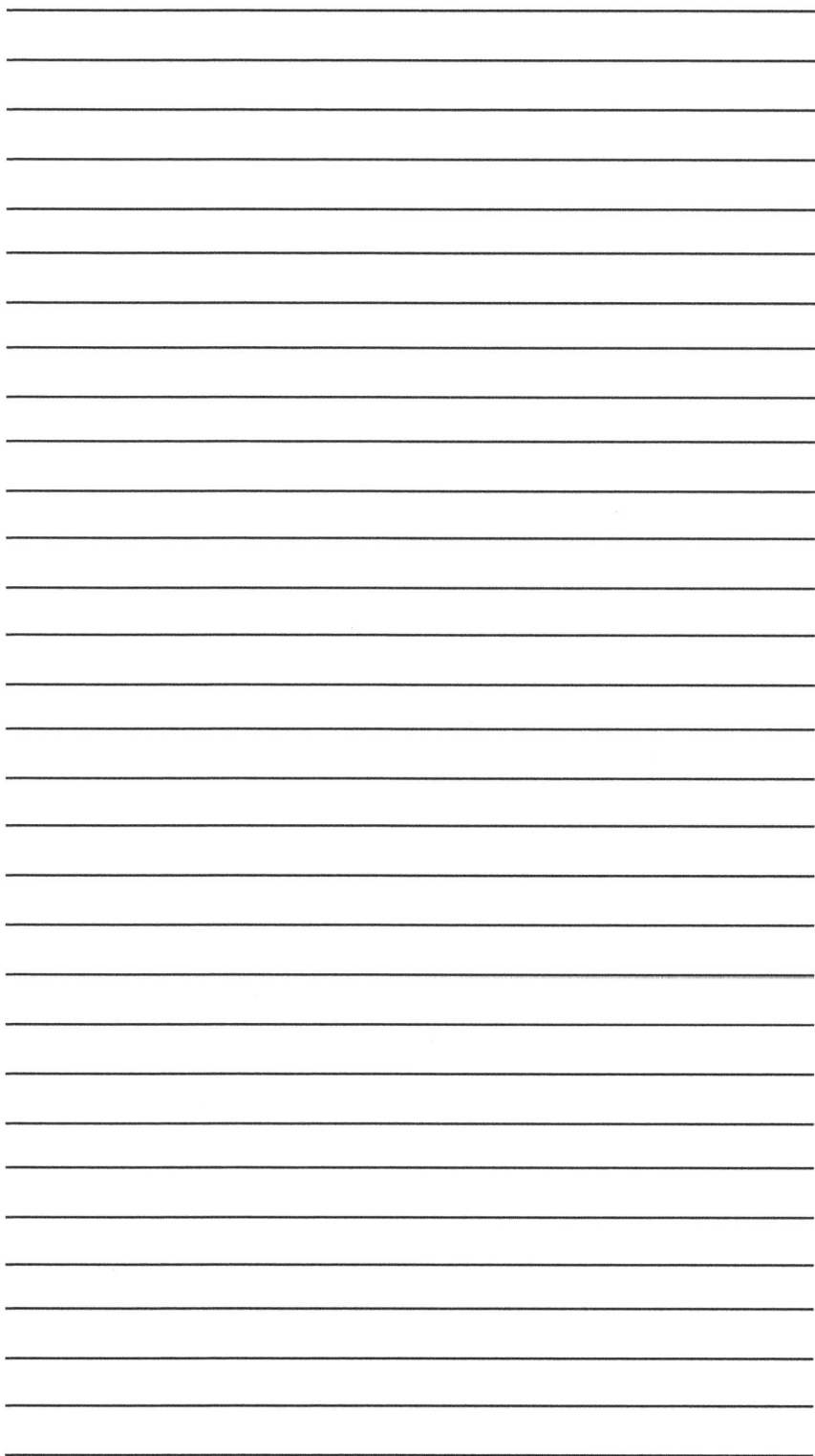

Adjust your Amazon Ads.

Profitable keywords:

_____

_____

_____

_____

_____

_____

_____

_____

_____

_____

_____

_____

Profitable targeted products:

_____

_____

_____

_____

_____

_____

_____

_____

_____

_____

_____

_____

Profitable categories:

_____

_____

_____

_____

_____

_____

Check the search terms of your auto ads and write down
the profitable keywords and products. Set up new ads with
those.

_____

_____

_____

_____

_____

_____

_____

_____

_____

_____

_____

_____

_____

_____

How are your Sponsored Brands or Sponsored Display ads performing?

_____

_____

_____

_____

_____

Collect and analyze recent reviews from Amazon, Goodreads, and other platforms. Write down comments and phrases you can use in your marketing campaign.

_____

_____

_____

_____

_____

_____

_____

_____

_____

_____

_____

_____

_____

_____

Research trending topics in children's literature and incorporate them into your blog and social media posts.

_____

_____

_____

_____

_____

_____

_____

_____

_____

Newsletter ideas:

_____

_____

_____

_____

_____

_____

_____

_____

_____

_____

Pitch your book to reading blogs or YouTube channels.

YouTube Channel / # of subscribers / email sent date/ answer/results (views and comments)

_____/_____ /_____
_____

_____/_____ /_____
_____

_____/_____ /_____
_____

_____/_____ /_____
_____

_____/_____ /_____
_____

_____/_____ /_____
_____

_____/_____ /_____
_____

_____/_____ /_____
_____

_____/_____ /_____
_____

Biggest accomplishment this month:	Next goal:
What turned out better than expected?	What needs improvement?
New things to try:	Task to focus on:

Use this space to jot down ideas, reminders, and reflections as you work through your tasks.

Celebrate your victories, but don't let them make you complacent.

Month _____/_____

To do list:	M	T	W

T	F	S	S

BUDGET

Month _____/_____

Expense	Planned	Actual

Monthly tasks:

Update your website and social media with testimonials from satisfied readers.

Follow up on influencers and bloggers.

Engage with your followers by replying to comments and messages. Also, engage with at least five other accounts by commenting on their posts or sharing their content.

Review the competition's ads for ideas and inspiration.
https://www.facebook.com/ads/library/
Write down ideas and inspirations:

_____

_____

_____

_____

_____

_____

_____

_____

_____

_____

_____

_____

_____

_____

Newsletter and blog ideas:

_____

_____

_____

_____

_____

_____

_____

_____

_____

_____

_____

_____

_____

_____

_____

_____

_____

_____

_____

_____

_____

_____

_____

_____

_____

_____

_____

_____

_____

_____

Create and schedule your social media posts for the month:

_____

_____

_____

_____

_____

_____

_____

_____

_____

_____

_____

_____

_____

_____

_____

_____

_____

_____

_____

_____

_____

_____

_____

_____

_____

_____

_____

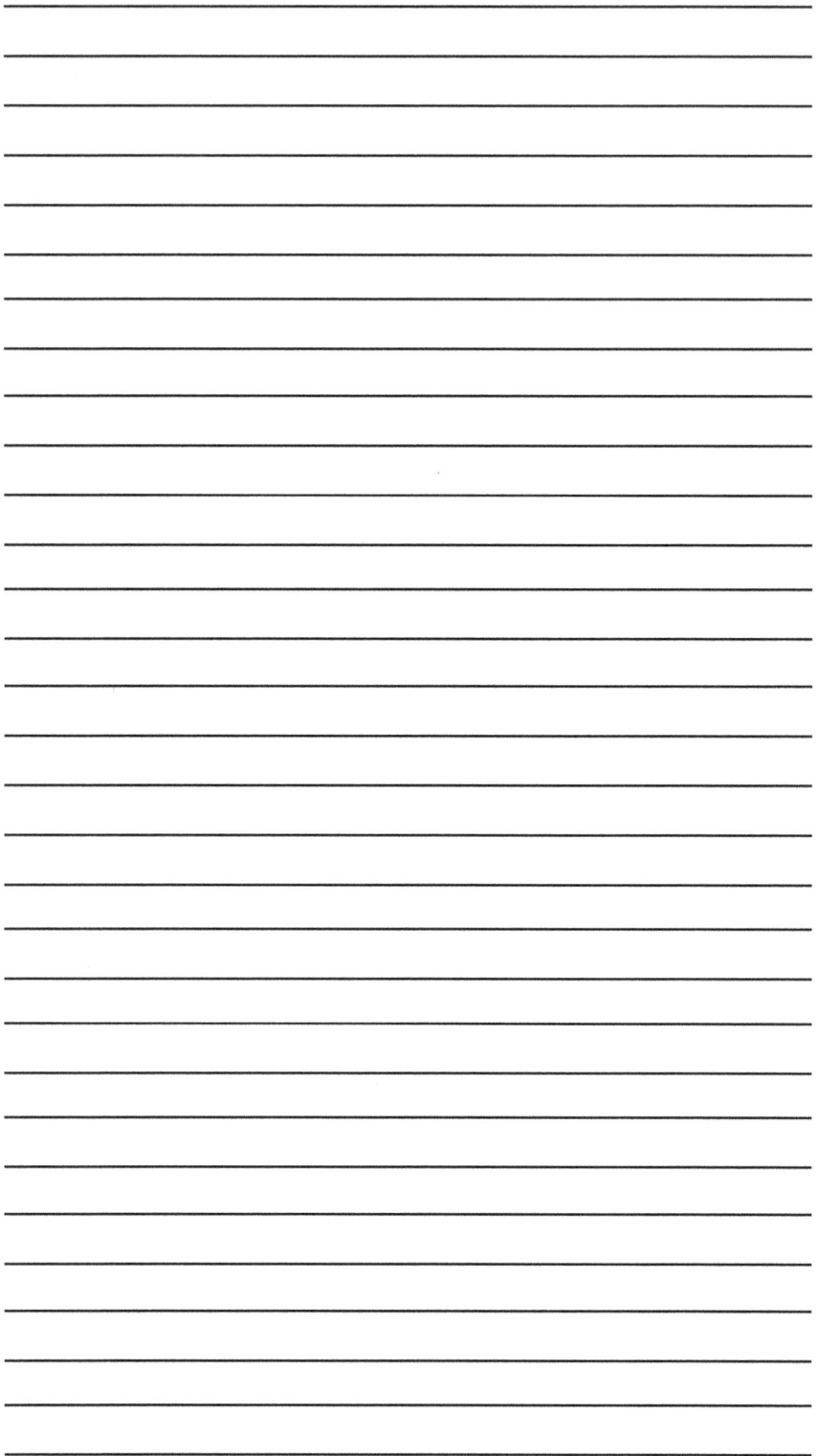

Adjust your Amazon Ads.

Profitable keywords:

_____
_____
_____
_____
_____
_____
_____
_____
_____
_____
_____

Profitable targeted products:

_____
_____
_____
_____
_____
_____
_____
_____
_____
_____
_____
_____

Profitable categories:

_____

_____

_____

_____

_____

_____

Other Profitable ads:

_____

_____

_____

_____

Check the search terms of your auto ads and write down the profitable keywords and products. Set up new ads with those.

_____

_____

_____

_____

_____

_____

_____

_____

Biggest accomplishment this month:	Next goal:
What turned out better than expected?	What needs improvement?
New things to try:	Task to focus on:

Use this space to jot down ideas, reminders, and reflections as you work through your tasks.

Well done! Your dedication and effort are inspiring.

Month _____/_____

To do list:	M	T	W

T	F	S	S

BUDGET

Month _____/_____

Expense	Planned	Actual

Monthly tasks:

Update your supplemental materials with new activity sheets or class lessons. Ideas:

_____

_____

_____

_____

_____

Engage with your followers by replying to comments and messages. Also, engage with at least five other accounts by commenting on their posts or sharing their content.

Identify social media accounts that are similar to yours. Analyze their performance and the most successful posts. What kinds of posts are the most popular?

_____

_____

_____

_____

_____

_____

_____

_____

_____

_____

_____

Brainstorm ideas for how to create similar content.

_____

_____

_____

_____

_____

_____

_____

_____

_____

_____

_____

_____

_____

_____

_____

_____

_____

_____

How are you different?

_____

_____

_____

_____

_____

Create and schedule your social media posts for the month:

_____

_____

_____

_____

_____

_____

_____

_____

_____

_____

_____

_____

_____

_____

_____

_____

_____

_____

_____

_____

_____

_____

_____

_____

_____

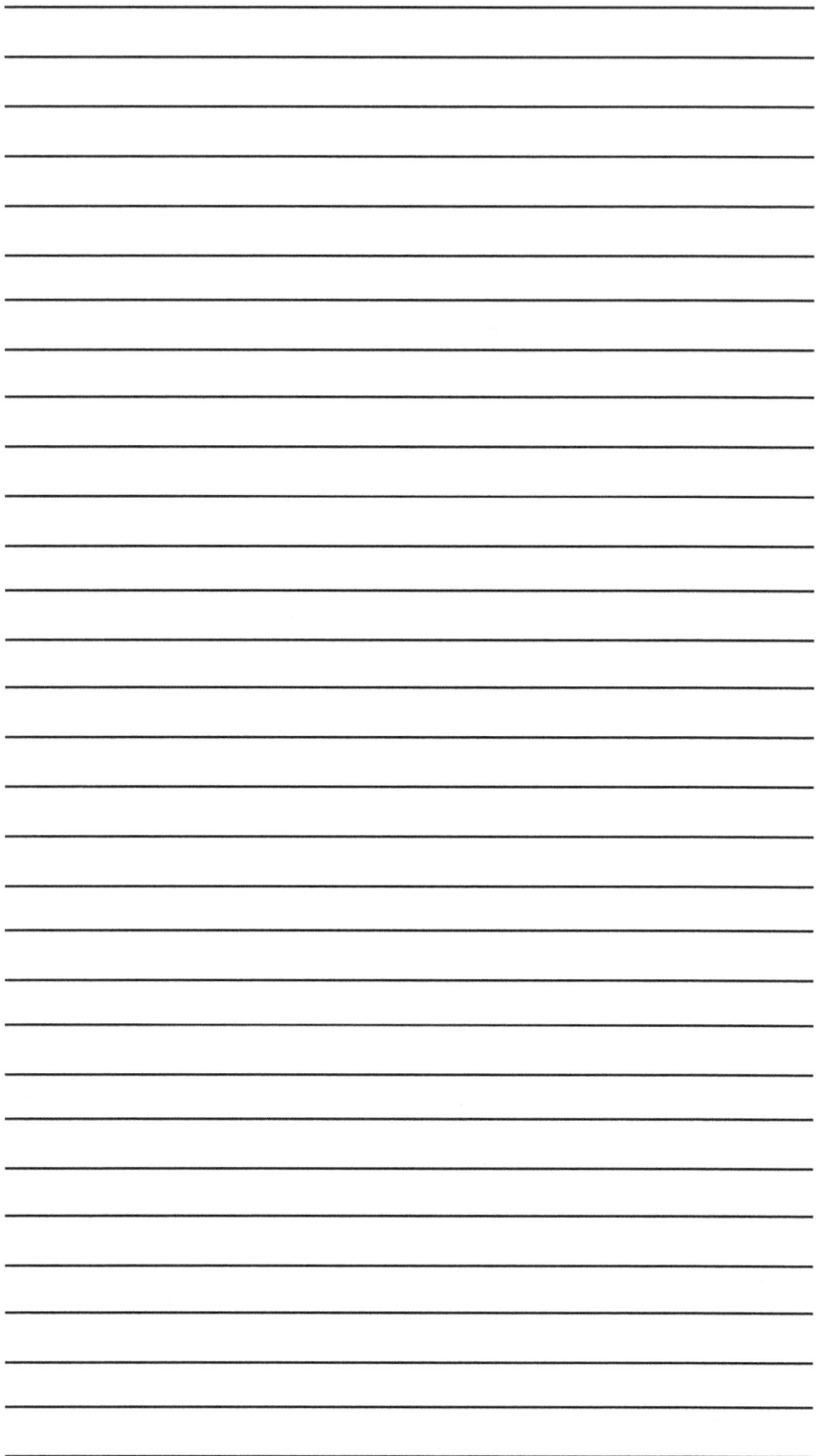

Adjust your Amazon Ads.

Profitable keywords:

_____

_____

_____

_____

_____

_____

_____

_____

_____

_____

_____

Profitable targeted products:

_____

_____

_____

_____

_____

_____

_____

_____

_____

_____

_____

_____

Profitable categories:

_____

_____

_____

_____

_____

Check the search terms of your auto ads and write down
the profitable keywords and products. Set up new ads with
those.

_____

_____

_____

_____

_____

_____

_____

_____

_____

_____

_____

_____

_____

_____

_____

Monitor how well your freebies are expanding your email list or boosting engagement. Evaluate the effectiveness of your email campaigns. Keep a record of the subject lines that achieve the highest open rates:

_____

_____

_____

_____

_____

_____

_____

Create and schedule your monthly newsletters using the information you gained from your analyses. Subject lines used:

_____

_____

_____

_____

_____

_____

_____

_____

_____

_____

_____

_____

Biggest accomplishment this month:	Next goal:
What turned out better than expected?	What needs improvement?
New things to try:	Task to focus on:

Use this space to jot down ideas, reminders, and reflections as you work through your tasks.

Reflect on your growth as an author and marketer, and celebrate your achievements!

_____

_____

_____

_____

_____

_____

_____

_____

_____

_____

_____

_____

_____

_____

_____

_____

_____

_____

_____

_____

_____

_____

_____

Keep up the great work and watch success follow you.

Write down three goals you want to accomplish within a year and actionable steps to achieve them:

_____

_____

_____

_____

_____

_____

_____

_____

_____

_____

_____

_____

_____

_____

_____

_____

_____

_____

Title of the book:

Genre and intended age group:

_____

What is your book about? What is the message?

_____
_____
_____
_____
_____
_____
_____

What do others say your book is about?

_____
_____
_____
_____
_____
_____
_____
_____
_____
_____

What problems does your book solve? How does it help readers?

_____

_____

_____

_____

_____

Does your book fit in a niche?

_____

_____

Do your "survey." Study your book's reviews on Amazon and Goodreads. Write down the positive comments and phrases readers say about your book.

_____

_____

_____

_____

_____

_____

_____

_____

_____

_____

_____

_____

Find successful books that are similar to yours and read their reviews. That will help you understand what buyers are looking for.

Title:_____ by:_____
Title:_____ by:_____
Title:_____ by:_____
Title:_____ by:_____
Title:_____ by:_____
Title:_____ by:_____
Title:_____ by:_____
Title:_____ by:_____
Title:_____ by:_____
Title:_____ by:_____

Write down positive comments and phrases used in the reviews of those books that can be used in your blurb:

_____

_____

_____

_____

_____

_____

_____

_____

_____

_____

_____

_____

What categories does your book fit in? Write down all categories and pick the best fit.

_____

_____

_____

_____

_____

_____

_____

_____

_____

_____

KDP Keywords:

_____

_____

_____

_____

_____

_____

_____

_____

_____

_____

_____

Notes:

Title of the book:

Genre and intended age group:

_____

What is your book about? What is the message?

_____
_____
_____
_____
_____
_____
_____

What do others say your book is about?

_____
_____
_____
_____
_____
_____
_____
_____
_____
_____
_____

What problems does your book solve? How does it help readers?

_____

_____

_____

_____

_____

Does your book fit in a niche?

_____

_____

Do your "survey." Study your book's reviews on Amazon and Goodreads. Write down the positive comments and phrases readers say about your book.

_____

_____

_____

_____

_____

_____

_____

_____

_____

_____

_____

_____

Find successful books that are similar to yours and read
their reviews. That will help you understand what buyers
are looking for.

Title:_____ by:_____

Title:_____ by:_____

Title:_____ by:_____

Title:_____ by:_____

Title:_____ by:_____

Title:_____ by:_____

Title:_____ by:_____

Title:_____ by:_____

Title:_____ by:_____

Title:_____ by:_____

Write down positive comments and phrases used in the
reviews of those books that can be used in your blurb:

_____

_____

_____

_____

_____

_____

_____

_____

_____

_____

_____

_____

What categories does your book fit in? Write down all categories and pick the best fit.

_____

_____

_____

_____

_____

_____

_____

_____

_____

_____

KDP Keywords:

_____

_____

_____

_____

_____

_____

_____

_____

_____

_____

_____

_____

Notes:

Title of the book:

Genre and intended age group:

_____

What is your book about? What is the message?

_____
_____
_____
_____
_____
_____
_____

What do others say your book is about?

_____
_____
_____
_____
_____
_____
_____
_____
_____
_____
_____

What problems does your book solve? How does it help readers?

_____

_____

_____

_____

_____

Does your book fit in a niche?

_____

_____

Do your "survey." Study your book's reviews on Amazon and Goodreads. Write down the positive comments and phrases readers say about your book.

_____

_____

_____

_____

_____

_____

_____

_____

_____

_____

_____

Find successful books that are similar to yours and read their reviews. That will help you understand what buyers are looking for.

Title:_____ by:_____
Title:_____ by:_____
Title:_____ by:_____
Title:_____ by:_____
Title:_____ by:_____
Title:_____ by:_____
Title:_____ by:_____
Title:_____ by:_____
Title:_____ by:_____
Title:_____ by:_____

Write down positive comments and phrases used in the reviews of those books that can be used in your blurb:

_____
_____
_____
_____
_____
_____
_____
_____
_____
_____
_____
_____

What categories does your book fit in? Write down all categories and pick the best fit.

_____

_____

_____

_____

_____

_____

_____

_____

_____

_____

KDP Keywords:

_____

_____

_____

_____

_____

_____

_____

_____

_____

_____

_____

_____

Notes:

_____

_____

_____

_____

_____

_____

_____

_____

_____

_____

_____

_____

_____

_____

_____

_____

_____

_____

_____

_____

_____

_____

_____

_____

_____

_____

Customer Persona:

Define your target audience. Give your customer persona a name (parent, teacher, etc.) What is their relationship to the child?

Child's interests:

_____
_____
_____
_____

Child's struggles:

_____
_____
_____

Customer's challenges:

_____
_____
_____

Customer's goals:

_____
_____
_____

Where do they get their recommendations from?

_____

_____

_____

Where do they shop?

_____

_____

_____

Preferred book features:

_____

_____

_____

_____

Other important information about your customer:

_____

_____

_____

_____

_____

_____

_____

_____

_____

Marketing message:

_____

_____

_____

_____

_____

_____

_____

_____

_____

_____

_____

_____

_____

_____

_____

_____

_____

_____

_____

_____

_____

_____

_____

_____

_____

_____

Customer Persona:

Define your target audience. Give your customer persona a name (parent, teacher, etc.) What is their relationship to the child?

Child's interests:

_____
_____
_____
_____

Child's struggles:

_____
_____
_____

Customer's challenges:

_____
_____
_____

Customer's goals:

_____
_____
_____

Where do they get their recommendations from?

_____

_____

_____

Where do they shop?

_____

_____

_____

Preferred book features:

_____

_____

_____

_____

Other important information about your customer:

_____

_____

_____

_____

_____

_____

_____

_____

_____

Marketing message:

_____

_____

_____

_____

_____

_____

_____

_____

_____

_____

_____

_____

_____

_____

_____

_____

_____

_____

_____

_____

_____

_____

_____

_____

_____

_____

Customer Persona:

Define your target audience. Give your customer persona a name (parent, teacher, etc.) What is their relationship to the child?

Child's interests:

_____
_____
_____
_____

Child's struggles:

_____
_____
_____

Customer's challenges:

_____
_____
_____

Customer's goals:

_____
_____
_____

Where do they get their recommendations from?

_____

_____

_____

Where do they shop?

_____

_____

_____

Preferred book features:

_____

_____

_____

_____

Other important information about your customer:

_____

_____

_____

_____

_____

_____

_____

_____

_____

Marketing message:

_____

_____

_____

_____

_____

_____

_____

_____

_____

_____

_____

_____

_____

_____

_____

_____

_____

_____

_____

_____

_____

_____

Notes:

Free downloadable templates:

https://www.dedonibooks.com/resources

If you find this planner helpful, please take a moment to share your experience by leaving a review.

I am not perfect and neither are my editors, mistakes might happen. If you find one, please reach out at diana@dedonibooks.com

www.ingramcontent.com/pod-product-compliance
Lightning Source LLC
Chambersburg PA
CBHW040850210326
41597CB00029B/4785